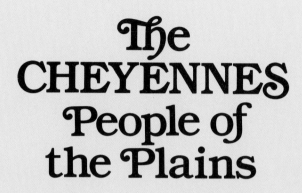

The CHEYENNES People of the Plains

NANCY BONVILLAIN

NATIVE AMERICANS
THE MILLBROOK PRESS
BROOKFIELD, CONNECTICUT

Library of Congress Cataloging-in-Publication Data
Bonvillain, Nancy.
The Cheyennes : people of the Plains / by Nancy Bonvillain.
        p.   cm. — (Native Americans)
Includes bibliographical references and index.
Summary: Examines the history, culture, way of life, and
contemporary problems of the Cheyennes, a Native American tribe that
dominated the Plains region in the nineteenth century.
ISBN 0-7613-0015-5 (lib. bdg.)
1. Cheyenne Indians — Juvenile literature. [1. Cheyenne Indians.
2. Indians of North America.] I. Title.   II. Series.
E99.C53B65   1996   970.004′97 — dc20   95-49929   CIP   AC

Cover: *Cheyenne Winter Games* by Walter Richard West,
courtesy of the Philbrook Museum of Art.
Photographs courtesy of The New York Public Library: pp. 11, 16 (Rare
Book Room), 21 (Rare Book Room), 23; The New York Public Library Picture
Collection: pp. 13, 19, 30, 42; Western History Collections, University of
Oklahoma Library: pp. 24 (#100, Campbell Collection), 48 (#37, Shuck
Collection); Museum of the American Indian: pp. 26, 46; National Museum of
American Art, Smithsonian Institution/Art Resource, New York: p. 27; Werner
Forman Archive/Art Resource, New York: pp. 35 (Peabody Museum, Salem,
Mass.), 38 (Private collection, New York); Denver Public Library, Western
History Department: p. 40; Colorado Historical Society: p. 43; Bettmann: p. 45;
John Warner: pp. 52, 55. Map by Joe LeMonnier.

Published by The Millbrook Press, Inc.
2 Old New Milford Road, Brookfield, Connecticut 06804

CONTENTS

The Cheyennes

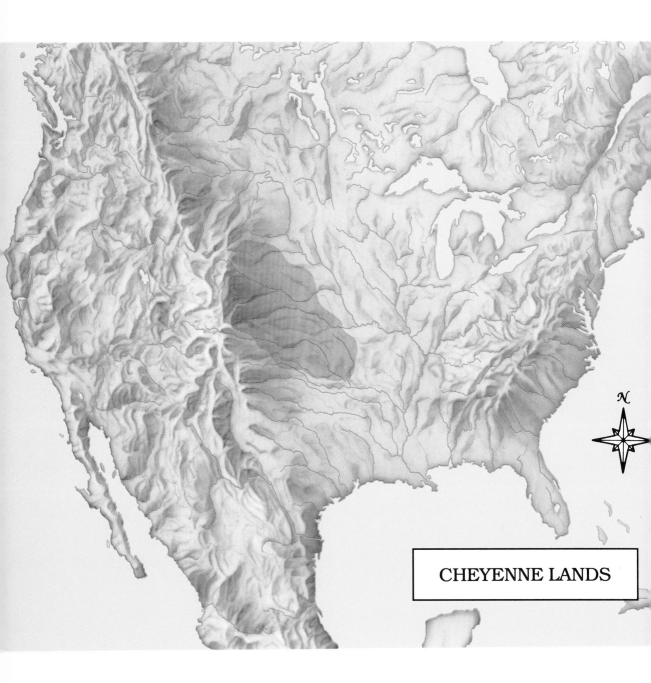

CHEYENNE LANDS

FACTS ABOUT
THE TRADITIONAL CHEYENNE
WAY OF LIFE

GROUP NAME:
Cheyenne;
Tsistsistas ("the people")

GEOGRAPHIC LOCATION:
North Dakota, South Dakota, Wyoming,
Colorado, Montana, Oklahoma

LANGUAGE FAMILY:
Algonquian

HOUSE TYPE:
Wooden lodge (before 1800); tepee (cone-shaped
home made of buffalo hides)

MAIN FOODS:
Buffalo, deer, wild potatoes,
turnips, berries, nuts

Chapter One

RENEWING THE SACRED MEDICINE ARROWS

The summer sun rises over the central plains of what is now the United States. It is the longest day of the year. One thousand Cheyenne families are putting up their tepees, cone-shaped homes made of buffalo skins. The tepees are arranged in a semicircular pattern, all with their doorways facing east toward the rising sun. The entire Cheyenne nation gathers here from their separate villages to celebrate their most sacred ceremony. They will renew the power of their Medicine Arrows. And they will renew the health, strength, and prosperity of the Cheyenne people.

The Cheyennes say that the ceremony was taught to them many years ago by Sweet Medicine, one of their beloved heroes, who learned it from the god Great Medicine. Great Medicine gave Sweet Medicine a bundle of four Sacred Arrows. Two arrows have power over buffalo and two have power over human beings. When the "buffalo arrows" are pointed at buffalo, the animals become weak and can easily be killed by hunters. And when the "human arrows" are pointed at enemies of the Cheyennes, the enemies lose their strength and can easily be defeated by Cheyenne warriors.

Sweet Medicine taught the Cheyennes a ceremony to renew the Arrows so that they would always have animals to eat and would always be able to defeat their enemies.

Following the teachings of Sweet Medicine, the Cheyenne nation celebrates their ritual and restores their Sacred Arrows. Sometime during the previous year, a man has made a holy vow to sponsor the ritual on behalf of his family and all Cheyenne people. In the springtime, the arrow-pledger, as he is called, travels to Cheyenne camps to announce the place and date for the ceremony. As the time draws near, each group leaves its camp and travels to the chosen location. They stop four times along the way to pray. When they arrive, women erect tepees for their families, and soon all are enjoying good food and the company of relatives and friends.

The Sacred Medicine Arrow Renewal lasts four days. On the first day, several tepees are erected in the middle of the ceremonial grounds. In the very center is a large tepee called the Sacred Arrow Lodge, where the religious leader known as the Arrow Keeper will perform the most solemn part of the ritual at sunrise on the second day.

As the rite begins, all other Cheyennes remain quiet in their tepees. The Arrow Keeper unwraps the bundle of animal skins holding the Sacred Arrows. If the Arrows are soiled or damaged, he must clean and repair them. The Arrow Keeper sings holy songs over the Arrows to renew their power.

Early in the morning of the third day, every family gives the Arrow Keeper a small stick made of willow. The Arrow Keeper

A dancer performs during the Sacred Medicine Arrow Renewal, an annual ceremony intended to renew the health, strength, and prosperity of the Cheyenne people.

holds each stick over a fire burning with sweet incense. As the smoke covers the stick, it is blessed. And as the stick is blessed, so is the family that it represents.

On the fourth and final day, the Arrows are displayed in the medicine lodge. All boys and men file through the lodge to view the Arrows and receive the powers that they will need when they go out hunting buffalo or are called to war to defend their families. As night falls, the Arrow Keeper and other religious leaders pray together, asking for spirit protection for their people.

And as the next dawn breaks, the Sacred Medicine Arrow ritual ends with the renewal of life, health, and prosperity for the nation. The people celebrate their good fortune with feasting and joyful reunions with relatives and friends.

CHEYENNE ORIGINS ▪ The Cheyennes are descendants of native peoples who are thought to have come into North America across frozen ice over the Bering Strait separating Alaska from the eastern coast of Russia. People began migrating across the frozen land perhaps thirty thousand years ago. They came in several waves, spread out over tens of thousands of years. It took many thousands of years for the descendants of these travelers to settle throughout North and South America. At first, most of the people followed a similar path, heading a short distance inland into Canada and then south along the valleys near the Rocky Mountains. Once they reached the northwestern United States, they spread in numerous directions.

Ancestors of the Cheyennes settled in the woodlands surrounding the Great Lakes. They were one of many groups of Native Americans known as Algonquians, from the name given to their family of related languages. No one knows exactly when people arrived in the region, but by the middle of the seventeenth century, the Cheyennes were well established in fertile valleys in Minnesota along the upper Mississippi River west of Lake Michigan and Lake Superior.

*The Cheyennes, who first flourished in the valleys
of the upper Mississippi near the Great Lakes,
were forced to move farther west into the central
plains as settlers from the East swarmed into their
lands. Here, Native Americans watch as the Pacific
Railroad cuts through their hunting grounds.*

■ 13 ■

From that location, the Cheyennes moved several times during the next 250 years. Their movements were part of a complex process that began shortly after Europeans arrived on the eastern shores of North America. As the number of Europeans increased, their desire for land and resources also grew. In order to get more land, they dislodged native peoples who had lived in North America for thousands of years. At first, Europeans killed or frightened away tribes living in the East. Survivors headed westward, hoping to find peace and security. But as they moved west, they entered territories occupied by other native peoples. And so a steady process of dislocations began, lasting several centuries and affecting hundreds of tribes.

By the seventeenth century, eastern groups came to Cheyenne territory in the upper Mississippi valley. The Cheyennes then began their migrations west into the central plains. In the nineteenth century, they were pushed even farther when American settlers arrived in Cheyenne lands. The presence of settlers caused conflicts over territory and resources that eventually led to the deaths of thousands of Cheyennes and the loss of their original homeland.

Chapter Two

THE CHEYENNES' HOMELAND

The recorded history of the Cheyennes begins in 1680 in Minnesota. At that time, a French explorer, Sieur de La Salle, was visited by members of a tribe he called the Chaa, later called the Cheyenne by the French. The word *Cheyenne* comes from the language of the Dakota, an Indian tribe who lived nearby in southern Minnesota. In the Dakota language, *Shahiyena* means "people who talk differently," or "foreigners." But Cheyennes' own name for themselves was *Tsistsistas*, meaning "human beings" or "people." It has often happened that the names by which Native Americans are known have not come from their own languages, but rather from languages of neighboring groups.

CHEYENNE VILLAGE LIFE ▪ When Cheyennes met La Salle, they had been living for a long time in villages in the wooded valleys of the Mississippi River and along the shores of nearby lakes. Their villages were small, having perhaps two or three hundred residents. They lived in sturdy houses built of wooden

The French explorer Sieur de La Salle, who traded with the Cheyennes in Minnesota, was killed in 1687 by members of his own expedition as they searched for the Mississippi River. This engraving by Louis Hennepin is entitled "The Sieur de La Salle unhappily assassinated."

frames covered with packed earth and bark from elm or birch trees. The number of villages is unknown, but European observers said that the Cheyennes were not a large tribe.

The most important food of the early Cheyennes was the wild rice that grew in abundance along the shores of lakes and in marshes near rivers and streams. Women gathered wild rice in summertime. They cooked some of the rice for summer meals but preserved most of it for use through the fall and winter by roasting the rice slowly over fire. In addition, women gathered many varieties of plants, including wild potatoes, turnips, acorns, blueberries, and raspberries.

Cheyenne men caught fish and turtles in nearby lakes and rivers. They hunted deer, rabbits, and other small animals in the dense woodlands. And they caught large quantities of ducks and geese.

The Cheyennes' way of living was well suited to their bountiful environment. But toward the end of the seventeenth century, Cheyennes began to leave the upper Midwest because of conflict with eastern and northern neighbors who themselves were being pushed westward by the increasing numbers of British and French traders and settlers in North America. Some of the Cheyennes' neighbors, such as the Dakotas, Crees, and Assiniboins, had gotten guns from European traders and were better equipped to fight than were the Cheyennes. Since the Cheyennes were unable to defend themselves, they left the region, hoping to find safety to the west.

LIVING ON THE PRAIRIES ▪ After several moves, Cheyennes arrived in eastern North Dakota and built villages along the Sheyenne River sometime in the early 1700s. Their new country in the northern prairies was rich with resources. Women gathered large quantities of wild potatoes, turnips, grasses, and berries. Men hunted numerous species of animals, including buffalo, elk, deer, raccoons, foxes, and bears. The rivers teemed with fish such as sturgeon, pike, and catfish. And thousands of birds, ducks, and geese appeared in the region.

In addition to natural resources, the Cheyennes began to grow some of their own food. Women were responsible for farming. They learned the techniques from native peoples nearby, such as the Otos, Mandans, Hidatsas, and Arikaras. Cheyennes grew several crops, mainly corn, beans, squash, and tobacco.

During their years on the prairies, the Cheyennes prospered. Farming, hunting, and gathering provided plenty of food. They used the hides of buffalo and deer to make clothing, bedding, bags, and containers. And they traded animal skins and meat to their neighbors the Mandans and Hidatsas for farm produce and utensils.

The Cheyennes lived in villages of various sizes. Some were small, containing two or three hundred people. Others were larger, with perhaps five or six hundred residents. They lived in lodges made of wood and covered with earth and bark. The lodges were spacious enough to house fifteen to thirty people of two, three, or more related families.

Even though the Cheyennes were content with their good life on the prairies, their security did not last long. By the middle of the eighteenth century, changes began to affect them that ended in their forced movement still farther west. In 1738, a French trader named Pierre La Vérendrye opened a trading post on the southern shores of Lake Winnipeg in the province of Manitoba, Canada, not far from Cheyenne territory. At first, the Cheyennes welcomed European traders from whom they got manufactured goods, such as metal tools and utensils, in exchange for buffalo hides and deerskins. They liked metal goods because the metal did not break or wear out as quickly as

*During their years on the prairie, the
Cheyennes lived in lodges similar to these, made
of wood and covered with earth and bark.*

traditional objects made of stone, bone, and wood. Cheyennes also traded for guns and ammunition that made hunting and warfare more effective.

Then, sometime after 1750, the Cheyennes made an important addition to their way of life when they began to trade for horses with western native peoples such as the Crows. The Crows got horses from Comanches and Utes who, in turn, got horses from Spanish traders located in the southwest. Horses were valuable because they made traveling and hunting easier. Instead of following animals on foot, hunters on horseback could cover a wide area. And horses could carry large quantities of meat and hides back to Cheyenne villages.

But by the late 1700s, conditions on the prairies worsened. Tribes from the East and Midwest were pushing into the central prairies because of increased pressure from Europeans and American colonists who were taking more and more land from native peoples. As the tribes moved westward, they once again came into Cheyenne territory. Too many people were competing for the natural resources of the region. As a result, warfare became more frequent. Once again Cheyennes left their villages, moving farther west. Once again, they hoped to find peace and security.

BEGINNING ANEW ON THE PLAINS ▪ In the early nineteenth century, Cheyennes built settlements west of the Missouri River on the plains of South Dakota. They spread west and south, expanding their territory to the Rocky Mountains in Montana, Wyoming, and Colorado. In this region, the Cheyennes established a way of life quite different from the one they left behind on the prairies. They no longer lived in permanent villages, but moved their camps several times each year. They no longer planted crops. Instead they hunted animals, especially buffalo, and gathered wild plants. And they no longer lived in peace. They had to defend their new homeland from American settlers who poured into the area in ever-increasing numbers.

"Buffalo Hunt Chase," by nineteenth-century artist
George Catlin, well known for his depictions of North
American Indians. The Cheyennes shown here are
hunting buffalo with spears and bows and arrows.

COMMUNITY LIFE

The Cheyennes' way of life on the plains was possible because of the horses they obtained through trade with Europeans. Cheyenne hunters on horseback covered a vast territory. The Cheyennes also used horses to carry their housing, clothing, and utensils when they traveled from one settlement to another.

Because of the great value of horses to their way of life, the Cheyennes measured a person's wealth in terms of the number of horses that he or she owned. Some individuals and families owned herds consisting of hundreds of horses, while others had only a few.

WOMEN'S WORK ■ Women performed many tasks including gathering wild foods, preparing meals, and furnishing their families with shelter and clothing.

Women collected wild plants, roots, seeds, grasses, and berries. Favorite foods included turnips, bulbs of lilies, prickly pears, milkweed buds, thistles, and chokecherries.

In the morning, groups of women left their villages carrying digging sticks to pry roots and plants out of the ground. Some

Women made good use of horses as pack animals. Here the women are collecting plants and digging roots. Hitched to the horse is a travois, a simple sledlike cart made from two poles and a platform.

plants were eaten within a few days, cooked in soups and stews. Others were dried in the sun to preserve them for future meals. Dried berries were also mixed with dried buffalo meat to make pemmican. Other meats and fish were roasted over fires or boiled in soups and stews.

Cheyenne women made the housing, furnishings, and clothing used by their families from buffalo or deer hides. The first task was softening the hides by a process known as tanning. The hide was scraped to remove fat and meat and then rubbed with a combination of animal brains and soapweed. After soaking overnight, it was cleaned, dried in the sun, and finally softened by being pulled back and forth over a thick rope of buffalo sinew. The hide was then ready to be sewn into useful objects.

The Cheyennes' shelter was a tepee, a cone-shaped structure made of buffalo hides. Small tepees required ten buffalo hides, while larger ones were made from as many as twenty.

This photograph from 1895 shows a summer encampment on the plains, where the Cheyennes lived in tepees. The meat hanging from the poles is drying in the air and sun so that it can be saved to eat in the winter.

After the hides were sewn together, they were placed over a frame of about twenty long wooden poles that were dug into the ground in a circular pattern. The tops of the poles were tied together and covered with another hide that could be opened to allow smoke from an interior cooking fire to exit the tepee. Furnishings consisted of mats made of grass and bedcovers made from buffalo hides.

Tepees were well suited to the Cheyennes' way of life. When people moved to new settlements several times each year, they quickly dismantled their tepees, rolled up the hides, and transported the tepees and all their belongings on a sledlike device called a *travois* that was pulled by their horses. When they arrived at a new location, the tepees were reassembled.

Women wore loose deerskin dresses that reached below the knees. Men wore breechcloths made from a square piece of animal skin hung in front from a cord tied around the waist. In cold weather, men also wore leggings that reached from the hip to the foot. And in winter, both women and men covered themselves with buffalo robes. Clothing was often decorated with embroidery of porcupine quills and small beads. Women who excelled in quillwork and had produced at least thirty garments could become members of the Robe-Quillers society. Their achievement was considered equal to that of warriors, and they were highly respected in their communities.

MEN'S WORK ▪ The major work of Cheyenne men was hunting large animals, especially buffalo that migrated in huge herds. They hunted antelope, deer, elk, and wild sheep as well. Men also caught numerous varieties of birds and fished in nearby rivers and streams.

*This deerskin shirt is decorated with beads,
porcupine quills, and fringe made from horsehair.*

During the fall and winter when animals were scarce, men usually hunted alone or with one or two companions. They used wooden bows, arrows, lances tipped with stone or iron, and rifles to down their prey, often after tracking them for hours or even days.

In summer, when buffalo formed huge herds, Cheyennes organized communal groups to hunt the animals. Hundreds of families left their spring camps and came together in a large settlement. Strict rules applied to hunters' activities. No one was allowed to hunt on his own for fear that his actions might frighten the buffalo and cause them to stampede off far in the distance. When the communal hunt began, all men left camp, rode on horseback to the buffalo herd, and attacked the animals. They sometimes drove the buffalo over a cliff where the animals fell to their death or were easily killed by hunters waiting below. Hundreds, even thousands, of buffalo were killed during a communal hunt.

Snowshoes helped the Cheyennes skim quickly across winter snowdrifts, which sometimes bogged down the buffalo and made them easier to hunt.

A Recipe for
Meatless Pemmican

In traditional times, the Cheyennes made pemmican from dried buffalo meat combined with nuts, dried fruits, and berries. Now pemmican can be made without meat. It is a tasty and nutritious treat. This recipe makes 12 servings.

Ingredients
- ½ cup cornmeal
- ½ cup raisins
- ½ cup peanuts
- ½ cup hickory nuts
- ½ cup dried apples
- ½ cup honey or maple syrup

Preparation
1. Spread cornmeal in a thin layer on a cookie sheet and place it in a warm oven (set at lowest possible setting) for 15 to 30 minutes. Check it frequently to make sure it doesn't burn. Take it out when it is completely dry.
2. Chop the raisins, nuts, and apples into very small pieces.
3. Combine the nuts, raisins, apples, and cornmeal.
4. Add the honey or maple syrup to the dry ingredients. Blend together.
5. Divide the mixture into ¼-cup portions and press them into small cakes. The cakes can be stored in the refrigerator and eaten when desired.

CHEYENNE FAMILIES ▪ Cheyennes lived in households of families linked by descent through women. Households often consisted of an elder couple, their unmarried children, and their married daughters and the daughters' husbands and children. The number of people belonging to a single household usually ranged from fifteen to thirty individuals.

In addition to their own households, people considered themselves related to other members of their mothers' and fathers' extended families. Every Cheyenne could depend on any of their numerous relatives for assistance in times of need. People generously gave their kin food and clothing and provided shelter during visits. When people were ill, their relatives helped the family with work and supplies. With this system of aid and cooperation, all Cheyennes were assured a decent lifestyle. No one lived in poverty or want when others had more resources.

TRIBAL GOVERNMENT ▪ The Cheyennes had a strong central government concerned with matters of peace and war. The Cheyenne nation consisted of ten separate groups or bands, each with its own territory and leaders. During most of the year, the bands lived in separate areas and went about their work independently. But on several occasions, especially for communal hunts and tribal ceremonies conducted in the summertime, the entire nation came together. The central government then played a major role in solving disputes within the tribe, planning communal activities, and discussing relations with other groups.

*Cheyenne households were large and extended,
sometimes including up to thirty people of all generations.
Everyone worked together to provide for the group.*

The central government consisted of peace leaders and warrior societies. The peace leaders formed a Council of Forty-Four. According to Cheyenne beliefs, the Council was begun long ago by a woman named Short Woman who wanted to end feuds and violence among the people. The Council was made up of forty-four chiefs who served for terms of ten years. Chiefs were older men who excelled in hunting and warfare. They were chosen for their intelligence, compassion, generosity, and even-tempered personalities. At the head of the Council were five sacred chiefs, chosen from among men who had already served on the body. One of these men was named the Sweet Medicine Chief and was considered to be the secular and religious head of the nation.

When the Council held meetings, all interested men and women could attend. All could voice their opinions, and the advice of all was seriously considered. After long debates, the Council made decisions with the people's approval.

The second branch of Cheyenne government consisted of five military societies, named the Swift Fox, Red Shield, Elk, Dog, and Bowstring. Young men could join any of the groups when they reached adulthood. The societies carried out the wishes of the Council of Forty-Four. In addition, during the summer buffalo hunts, they functioned as police to make sure that all hunters obeyed the rules. They also defended the encampment against attack from enemies.

The military societies also organized large war parties, numbering more than a hundred fighters, in raids against their foes. Participation was completely voluntary, but there was strong social pressure for young men to join war parties.

The more common type of warfare was conducted by small groups who banded together under the leadership of an experienced warrior. Men joined if they thought well of the plans and objectives. Such raids usually had the goal of stealing enemies' horses. Cheyenne raiding parties approached enemy camps at night or early in the morning. They cut the enemies' horses loose and quickly retreated with their booty.

The Cheyennes gave great respect to successful and courageous warriors. Men who performed daring deeds in war, stole many horses, and avenged the deaths of their comrades had high prestige in their communities.

Chapter Four

THE RELIGIOUS WORLD
OF THE CHEYENNES

The Cheyennes' religious beliefs stressed the importance of both individual spiritual experience and community participation. Individuals sought personal contact with the supernatural realm. Families conducted rituals for their members at birth, puberty, marriage, and death. And the entire Cheyenne nation gathered together for grand religious celebrations.

THE CHEYENNE WORLD ▪ According to Cheyenne belief, the universe consisted of a number of layers of existence. The Earth itself had two layers. The Earth's surface was a thin covering, only deep enough to contain the roots of plants and trees. The second Earth layer, called "Deep Earth," continued far below the surface. In it resided a female deity who gave the Earth its female character. Above the Earth was a layer of air that made breathing and life possible. Above the air layer was a realm called "Nearer Sky Space" for clouds, winds, and holy places on tops of mountains. At the very top was "Blue Sky Space" where the sun, moon, and stars existed. A male deity resided in the Blue Sky Space and gave the sky its male character.

Many different deities lived in the universe. Some were associated with the sun, moon, stars, winds, clouds, and thunder. Others were linked to the four cardinal directions of east, south, west, and north. And some lived in mountains, streams, caves, and other locations.

CONTACT WITH THE SPIRIT WORLD ▪ The Cheyennes believed that all spirits could affect human life. Spirits protected people from harm, cured illness, and brought good fortune. But they also caused disease, death, and misfortune. And, of course, they had knowledge and abilities far superior to those of human beings. People tried to honor and please the spirits so that they would act kindly and give blessings, knowledge, good health, and success.

The Cheyennes said that all people could have direct contact with the spirit world. Spirits might appear to people in dreams when sleeping or in visions while awake. When they appeared, they might look like animals or birds or they might appear as wind or light. And they might have the shape of human beings.

People contacted spirits to gain knowledge, power, and the ability to heal or foretell the future. Although any man or woman could seek a spirit's aid, mature men were most likely to do so. The seeker left the village and went alone into the hills to pray and wait, usually for four days. The seeker wore little clothing, ate nothing, and did not sleep during the time of the ordeal. If the seeker's prayers were answered, a spirit appeared and bestowed knowledge. It gave a special song that the person could sing whenever he or she was in danger or needed advice.

Cheyenne Sign Language

In the nineteenth century, the Cheyennes communicated with other Native American peoples of the plains by means of a sign language. The people developed this system so that they could communicate with members of other tribes whose spoken language they did not understand. Sign language contained many gestures that conveyed specific meanings. For example,

cold: clench both hands and cross the forearms in front of the chest with a trembling motion

rain (or *snow*): hold out the hands at the level of the shoulder with the palms facing down and with the fingers hanging down, then push the hands in a downward direction

chief: raise the forefinger pointing upward, then reverse the finger and bring it down

This whistle made from eagle bone was used during ceremonies and rituals. The whistle was held in the dancer's teeth and helped the dancer fall into a trance-like state.

And the spirit often gave the seeker an object that contained power, such as a bird's feather, an animal bone, or a stone of unusual shape. The person carried the sacred object in a small pouch so as to always have the spirit's protection.

FAMILY CEREMONIES ▪ Cheyenne families held ceremonies to celebrate happy events such as birth, puberty, and marriage, and to mourn the deaths of their loved ones.

Cheyenne women gave birth either in their home tepees or in a special birth lodge. They were attended by midwives and by healers who sang sacred songs if the mother's labor was long and difficult. After the baby's umbilical cord was cut, the mother dried it and saved it in a small pouch. The child kept the bag until he or she grew up because the Cheyennes believed that the umbilical cord contained some essence of the child's personality.

When a young girl had her first menstruation, her father called out the happy news to the entire camp. The pubescent girl was bathed and painted with red paint by older female relatives before she entered a special hut where she remained for four days in the company of her grandmother, who taught her the duties of adult women.

Cheyennes celebrated marriages with an exchange of gifts between the families of husband and wife. When a couple wished to marry, the man's relatives brought as many gifts of clothing, ornaments, and horses as they could afford to the woman's home. If the woman's family agreed to the marriage, they distributed the gifts among their relatives. The next day, they collected presents of equal value to give to the young man's family. The bride, dressed in her finest clothing, rode to her husband's home, accompanied by her kin. Afterward, all in attendance joined in a joyful feast.

Cheyennes marked a person's death with a solemn funeral and long periods of mourning. They believed that when a person died, the soul or spiritual essence left the body and traveled to the Blue Sky Space along a path of stars called the "Hanging Road" (the Milky Way). There the soul joined all others who had died before. The souls live in peace, pursuing the daily activities that they had enjoyed on earth.

Burials took place soon after death. Relatives of the deceased dressed the body in fine clothing and wrapped it in buffalo robes. It was carried out of the village and either covered with rocks on the ground or placed on a scaffold suspended from a tree. Small tools or utensils were left with the body so that the soul might use them in the afterworld.

Relatives, especially wives and mothers of the deceased, mourned deeply for as long as one year. They cut their hair, gashed their foreheads with knives, and lived in isolation for a time. Men also mourned deaths of their kin, but generally for shorter periods.

TRIBAL CEREMONIES ▪ The Cheyenne nation performed ceremonies to renew their life, strength, and good fortune. These rituals, including the Sacred Medicine Arrow Renewal and the Sun Dance, also aimed to strengthen the balance of nature and the harmony that exists among all of the world's creatures.

Sun Dances were held every summer to restore the resources of the Earth so that people and other living creatures could survive. It was a ritual held by nearly all native peoples of the plains, but each tribe had its own particular version. According to Cheyenne belief, long ago when people were starving and no food was to be found, a hero named Erect Horns went with a woman companion in search of animals and plants. They were met by a holy spirit who taught them the Sun Dance. When they returned to their people, they performed the ceremony and restored the Earth's bounty.

The Cheyenne Sun Dance lasted eight days. During the first four days, the people built a Great Medicine Lodge around a sacred center pole selected by one of the bravest warriors. Inside the lodge, religious leaders sang songs to renew the Earth.

The last four days were devoted to dancing by men who had pledged to sacrifice themselves in the presence of the spirits. The dancers pierced the skin on their chests, backs, or arms and inserted small bone skewers tied to long ropes suspended

A depiction of the Sun Dance, painted on cloth by a Native American artist. Photographs of this sacred ceremony are not allowed to be published.

from a pole erected in the center of the dance grounds. As they danced slowly back and forth toward the pole, small pieces of skin gradually pulled away. All the while, the dancers prayed to spirits while onlookers beat drums and sang songs. Men who danced earned great respect for their willingness to endure pain in order to honor the spirits.

■ ■ ■

Cheyenne rituals emphasized the importance of balance and harmony in the world. And they stressed the role of each member of society in the well-being of all.

Chapter Five

THE DISPOSSESSED

During the early nineteenth century, the Cheyennes had a secure way of life. They had abundant resources and they traded with other native peoples living nearby, including the Crows, Arapahos, and Kiowas. But beginning around 1830, inroads by American settlers began a process that destroyed the Cheyennes' homeland.

In the early 1830s, Charles and William Bent opened a trading post in Colorado on the southern fringe of Cheyenne territory. Several Cheyenne bands moved near Bent's post so that they could trade there. The Cheyenne gave buffalo meat and hides in exchange for metal tools, utensils, and guns.

American and European companies also traded with the Cheyennes for buffalo bones that were ground into powder for use in making bone china dishes.

SETTLERS INVADE CHEYENNE LANDS ■ Although Cheyennes benefited from trade, the growing white presence in the plains eventually led to disaster. By 1850, Santa Fe, New Mexico,

*Although the invasion of settlers from the East
threatened the Cheyennes, trading posts like
Bent's Fort in Colorado gave the Cheyennes a way to
trade buffalo meat and bones for tools and guns.*

became an important center of commerce, attracting many traders and settlers who traveled through Cheyenne hunting territory. And when gold was discovered in California, new trails opened up through the center of Cheyenne lands. Thousands of traders, prospectors, and settlers streamed into Cheyenne territory.

In 1851, the United States government proposed a treaty to establish peace with the largest plains tribes, including the

Cheyennes, Lakótas, Arapahos, Crows, and Shoshones. Officials wanted to set definite boundaries for each tribe. By terms of the Fort Laramie Treaty, Cheyenne bands were permanently divided into two separate groups, the Northern Cheyennes and the Southern Cheyennes. Officials also wanted Native Americans to allow non-Indians to cross their lands. In return, the government promised to protect the Cheyennes from settlers.

The Fort Laramie Treaty was the first of many land treaties signed between Cheyennes and the United States. But despite official promises, the government never protected the Cheyennes from settlers who occupied their land. In fact, the U.S. Army defended the settlers and attacked the Cheyennes who resisted the theft of their land and resources.

After gold was discovered in the Rocky Mountains in 1858, more than 100,000 prospectors and settlers poured into Cheyenne territory to reach the mountains. They built mines and towns and harassed Indians living nearby. In 1861, the government forced the Cheyennes to sign a new treaty, called the Fort Wise Treaty, giving up the western portion of their territory in exchange for $450,000. But settlers continued to encroach on Cheyenne land. Whenever the Cheyennes resisted, they were attacked by local militias or the U.S. Army.

WAR COMES TO THE CHEYENNES ▪ As tensions mounted, Cheyenne peace chiefs tried to negotiate a truce with American leaders. But officials in Colorado wanted instead to annihilate the Cheyenne people. They set about a campaign to find and destroy native villages. On November 28, 1864, troops led by Colonel John Chivington came upon a Cheyenne camp at Sand

Creek headed by Chief Black Kettle. At dawn the next morning, 700 soldiers attacked the camp with rifles and cannons. At day's end, more than 400 Cheyennes were massacred. Their bodies were mutilated by the soldiers. Two thirds of the victims were women and children.

Black Kettle survived the massacre and quickly organized warriors to defend their remaining tribespeople. They won the support of other native groups such as the Lakotas and Arap-

Thousands of prospectors rushed west when gold was discovered in the Rocky Mountains in 1858. The route to the mountains took the settlers and their wagons and animals directly through Cheyenne territory.

In 1864 the U.S. Army attacked a camp of Cheyennes at Sand Creek in Colorado. In what came to be known as the Sand Creek Massacre, 400 Cheyennes were killed as they slept.

ahos. Hundreds of warriors raided American settlements, trading posts, and army units in Colorado. In one confrontation, the Cheyennes wiped out an entire army command.

After the end of the Civil War, the government turned its attention to expansion into the West. They wanted to force Native American tribes to abandon their traditional way of life, give up most of their territory, and settle on small reservations. The government wanted to provide land for settlers to build farms, ranches, and towns.

In 1867, leaders of the Southern Cheyennes signed a treaty, called the Treaty of Medicine Lodge Creek, giving up their land and agreeing to move to what was then called Indian Territory, now the state of Oklahoma. There the Cheyennes established a joint reservation for themselves and the Arapahos, another plains tribe who also lost their ancestral homeland. In exchange for their land, the Cheyennes received $500,000. The government also promised to give supplies of clothing and food for twenty-five years.

In the northern plains, conflicts occurred between settlers and the Northern Cheyennes. After 1874, when gold was discovered in the Black Hills of South Dakota in the eastern region of Cheyenne territory, thousands of miners and settlers poured into the area. The Cheyennes, vowing to resist the loss of their land, attacked mining camps. The government sent in soldiers to protect white expansion into Indian territory. After the Seventh Cavalry, led by General George Custer, attacked Cheyenne camps, the Cheyennes planned retaliation. With the support of Lakota warriors, they defeated Custer's troops in the Battle of the Little Bighorn on June 25, 1876. Custer and all of his 225 soldiers were killed.

Although the battle was a stunning victory for the Northern Cheyennes, their good fortune did not last long. The government sent thousands of soldiers to rid the plains of its original inhabitants to make way for settlers. Troops attacked several Cheyenne villages, killing most of the residents. In the end, Cheyenne leaders realized that they could not stop the tide of foreigners into their lands. To save the lives of their people, in 1877 they agreed to move to "Indian Territory" and live on a portion of the Southern Cheyenne reservation.

The Battle of Little Bighorn, in which General George Custer and all his soldiers were killed, was the last great victory for the Cheyennes. This drawing, illustrating the army's defeat, was made by a Cheyenne artist named White Bird in the late 1800s.

Most of the Cheyennes were resigned to their fate, but about one third of the Northern bands vowed to leave the reservation and return to their homeland. Led by Chief Morning Star (who was also known by the name Dull Knife) and Chief Little Wolf, a group of 85 warriors and 250 women and children headed north. They fought when they had to and successfully escaped the clutches of 17,000 soldiers sent to capture them. Although Little Wolf's band was captured, Morning Star's

Cheyenne leaders Morning Star (left) *and Little Wolf* (seated) *in the 1870s. Both later tried unsuccessfully to escape the reservation and return to their homeland.*

group remained free for several months. But they, too, were finally captured and sent to Fort Robinson in Nebraska. When they were told that they would be taken back to Oklahoma, they broke out of their barracks and fled into the hills. Soldiers pursued them, killing nearly half of the 150 men, women, and children in Morning Star's band.

ADJUSTING TO RESERVATION LIFE ▪ Life on the reservations was difficult. Cheyennes were no longer able to hunt buffalo and live where they wanted on the open plains. In Oklahoma, the Southern Cheyennes lived with their neighbors the Arapahos on a reservation of 4 million acres. The land there was dry and the resources were few. The people faced poverty, starvation, and disease. Without independent resources, Cheyennes had to rely on the federal government to keep the promises it made to supply the people with food and clothing. But the rations delivered were not nearly enough to feed and clothe the population.

Officials responded to the desperate situation by trying to make Cheyenne men become farmers. Most of the men resisted. Even those who tried to farm failed because of the poor quality of the soil, bad weather, and lack of farming equipment. The government then decided to lease much of the Cheyenne/ Arapaho reservation to American ranchers. But since land was rented so cheaply, at a rate of only two cents per acre per year, the Cheyennes never profited from the arrangement.

American authorities next turned to education to change the Cheyennes' values and ways of living. They sent children to boarding schools to separate them from their parents and their traditions. Girls and boys were forced to attend schools run by missionaries who taught them American values and Christian beliefs. In the summertime, children were sent to work as domestics and farmhands for American settlers.

Then, in 1887, the U.S. Congress passed a law, known as the General Allotment Act, that destroyed many Indian reservations, including that of the Southern Cheyennes, by forcing

Religious missionaries like the Mennonites opened schools to teach Native Americans, both children and adults, to speak and read English.

native people to give up their traditional culture and adopt American practices. The act divided reservation land into individual parcels or "allotments." Each family was assigned an allotment of 160 acres. Land that remained unassigned after all families had been given a parcel was then open to homesteading by settlers. After the act went into effect, the Southern Cheyenne/Arapaho reservation of 4 million acres decreased to only 529,692 acres.

As a result of years of government interference, the Southern Cheyennes lost most of their land and their traditional way of life. During this period, the Northern Cheyennes lived on a reservation of about 371,200 acres in Montana that was established in 1884. They took up farming and managed to survive on their land. But they, too, were affected by the influx of settlers late in the nineteenth century. Some Cheyennes sold hay and firewood to ranchers and worked in small towns that were built nearby.

As the nineteenth century ended, the Cheyenne nation was divided into two groups living on separate reservations. Their common path had been broken by government policies, but their common heritage, traditions, and hopes for the future remained strong.

Chapter Six

THE CHEYENNES
TODAY

The lives of the Cheyennes have continued to change in the twentieth century. For the Southern bands, changes have been more rapid and have had more negative results than for the Northern people. Still, both groups try to maintain some of their valued traditions.

THE SOUTHERN CHEYENNES ▪ After the Southern Cheyenne/Arapaho reservation was broken up into separate parcels of land, the tribal unit no longer existed. The vast majority of land, about 3.5 million acres, was not owned by Cheyenne or Arapaho residents at all, but by non-Indian farmers and ranchers. Some people tried to farm the small amount of land that they owned, but they had great difficulty because of the poor quality of the land, bad weather conditions, and lack of money to buy modern equipment. In contrast, the non-Indian Americans who bought the Cheyennes' land were much wealthier and could afford new farm machinery and large herds of animals.

Because they were poor, many Cheyenne families sold their land or rented it to farmers and ranchers. They tried to find work in nearby towns, but most people were not able to find good jobs. Because there were few local opportunities for work or income, people gave up their homes and left the area, hoping to do better elsewhere in Oklahoma or farther away throughout the United States.

The Cheyennes are steadily losing their land through sales of allotments to outsiders. When the original reservation of 4 million acres was allotted, the Cheyennes and Arapahos received only 562,000 acres. They now own less than 100,000 acres. In 1990, a nationwide census reported a total of 6,715 Native American people living in the area once known as the Cheyenne/Arapaho Reservation. (The census does not list people as Cheyenne or Arapaho but lists them together as "Native.") The same area now has 144,111 non-Indian residents.

THE NORTHERN CHEYENNES ▪ The Northern Cheyennes have held on to most of their original reservation in Montana. Although the reservation was divided into family allotments in 1926, the land that remained unassigned was not opened to outsiders, unlike the situation in Oklahoma. Instead, unassigned plots were put into the ownership of the tribe as a whole.

As a result of the secure land base, the population has steadily increased. In 1990, the reservation was home to 3,542 Cheyennes. The people use their land to graze herds of cattle for sale. And some people own or work in small local businesses such as stores, restaurants, and gas stations.

U.S. GOVERNMENT POLICIES ▪ Government policy toward Native Americans began a new direction in the 1930s as part of the New Deal programs of President Franklin Roosevelt. In 1934, Congress passed a law called the Indian Reorganization Act (IRA). The IRA gave funds to native tribes to buy back land that they had lost in sales to outsiders. The Northern Chey-

Today, government funding has created integrated schools for educating Native Americans, like this one in Ashland, Montana.

ennes are buying land that comes up for sale and holding it in communal ownership by the tribe. Today, in fact, the majority of the reservation (some 270,000 acres) is owned by the tribe while about 164,000 acres are owned by Cheyenne families. The Northern Cheyennes are hoping to buy back all land that had been lost to outsiders.

The IRA also outlined procedures for tribes to establish some degree of local self-government. Under this provision, both the Northern and Southern Cheyennes set up Tribal Councils with members elected by residents. The councils discuss local issues and develop programs for their people.

Another important step in correcting wrongs of the past was taken in 1947, when Congress passed the Indian Claims Act. The act enabled native tribes to sue the federal government for payment for land that had been taken illegally or for land that the government had bought at prices that were too low. In 1961, the Court of Indian Claims ruled that the government cheated the Cheyennes in 1865 when they paid only $1,162,000 for the people's land. The court stated that the land had been worth more than $23 million. As a result, both the Northern and Southern bands were each paid slightly more than $10 million to settle the claim. The Tribal Councils of both groups gave all tribal members some small cash payments and invested the rest in a fund for development projects in their communities and for student aid programs.

COAL IN MONTANA ▪ In the 1960s, deposits of some 5 billion tons of coal were discovered in the Northern Cheyennes' reservation. At first, the Cheyenne Tribal Council agreed to allow

American companies to mine the coal, but in 1974 they decided against the project because they were afraid that their land would be ruined by strip-mining, a process that extracts coal from below the surface and destroys the soil so that it cannot be used for farming or grazing animals. The coal companies fought the Council's decision, but a federal appeals court in Montana ruled that the Cheyennes had the right to stop mining on their land. The Cheyennes prefer to give up money from the coal companies so that they can protect the land as nature has given it to them. Indeed, they consider it their sacred duty to protect the land they believe represents the blood of their ancestors.

CHEYENNE TRADITIONS ▪ Much has changed in the lives of the Southern and Northern Cheyennes since their ancestors roamed the plains and prospered from their hunting, gathering, and trading. They now live in places far from their original homeland. Their income comes from ranching or from public and private jobs. Their political system has been altered. But they are all proud of their heritage and try to maintain some of their traditions. Many Cheyennes speak their own native language and learn about their unique history. And many people follow their traditional religious beliefs and practices.

The ancient ceremonies of community and world rebirth, the Sacred Medicine Arrow Renewal and the Sun Dance, are performed by religious leaders and attended by many tribal members. Large numbers of people join in the celebration of the renewal of the earth and its bounty. When the Sacred Medicine Arrows are displayed by the Arrow Keeper, the Cheyenne families are blessed, and the unity of all the Cheyenne people is celebrated.

Many Cheyennes gather each year to participate in traditional ceremonies of community and renewal of the Earth's resources. Here, a Cheyenne child performs a dance in full Native American dress.

A CHEYENNE STORY:
ORIGIN OF THE COUNCIL
OF FORTY-FOUR

Long ago, a girl named Short Woman lived with her parents and her brother on the plains at a distance from a large Cheyenne camp. One day the father, named Bull Looks Back, killed his wife and deserted his two young children. The children wandered about for a time trying to find the main camp to seek shelter and food. Finally, they came upon the camp and entered a lodge. There they were told that they were the children of Bull Looks Back, who was then also in the camp. When the father heard that his children had arrived, he said aloud: "Those monstrous children of mine killed their own mother and ate her flesh. That is why I left them. They should be staked to the ground and abandoned."

And so the people did as he said. The girl and boy were bound by leather ropes and left to die on the plains. But a dog approached at nightfall and chewed on the straps binding the girl. When she got free, she untied her brother and both ran swiftly away. They were met by a stranger who told them that the girl had a power to kill buffalo by looking at them. At first she did not believe the stranger's words, but when a large herd of buffalo appeared, she looked up and they all fell dead.

After she butchered the animals, the girl told a crow to carry some meat to the Cheyenne camp where she and her brother had been abandoned. She said to the crow: "Tell those people the meat is from the children they left on the plains to die." The people then understood that the children were alive and that the girl had special powers.

Then the girl sent for the people to come to her. She told them, "We are going to make chiefs. You know I have been accused of killing my mother. That is not true. Now, we shall make chiefs, and hereafter we shall have a rule that if anyone kills a fellow tribesmember they shall be ordered away from one to five years, whatever the people shall decide."

The girl chose the first chiefs. She told them, "You will swear that you will be honest and care for all the tribe."

The girl told the chiefs how they should act and gave them a pipe of peace to smoke. She taught them songs and prayers to guide and protect them. Then she said, "My brother and I will leave this earth. We may go up into the heavens. Yet I shall always be working for the people. I may be a star."

IMPORTANT DATES

c. 1700   Cheyennes leave their ancestral homeland in the upper Mississippi River valley in Minnesota and head west into the prairies of eastern North and South Dakota.

1738   French trader Pierre La Vérendrye opens a trading post on Lake Winnipeg near Cheyenne territory.

c. 1750   Cheyennes acquire horses through trade with the Crows.

c. 1800   Cheyennes move west from the prairies onto the plains of western South Dakota, extending their territory west to Colorado, Wyoming, and Montana.

1830s   Charles and William Bent open a trading post in Colorado, attracting trade and settlement by some Southern Cheyenne bands.

1849   Discovery of gold in California; increased numbers of American miners and settlers cross through Cheyenne territory.

1851   Treaty of Fort Laramie; Cheyennes agree to permanent division of their nation into Southern and Northern groups, and agree to allow non-Indians to cross their lands in exchange for promises of government protection from settlers.

1858   Discovery of gold in Rocky Mountains; more than 100,000 miners and settlers enter Cheyenne territory.

1861   Treaty of Fort Wise; Southern Cheyennes agree to give up the western portion of their territory in exchange for $450,000 and promises of protection from illegal settlement by non-Indians.

1864	Massacre of at least 400 Cheyenne men, women, and children at village of Sand Creek by American soldiers.
1867	Treaty of Medicine Lodge Creek; Southern Cheyennes agree to give up all their remaining land and move to a reservation in "Indian Territory" (now Oklahoma); Cheyennes agree to share the reservation with Arapahos; U.S. government gives Cheyennes $500,000 and promises of protection.
1876	Northern Cheyennes and Lakotas defeat General George Custer and his Seventh Cavalry in the Battle of the Little Big Horn.
1878	Northern Cheyennes agree to give up their land and move to the Southern Cheyenne reservation in Oklahoma.
1878	Northern bands under Morning Star (also known as Dull Knife) and Little Wolf leave the reservation and head north to their ancestral lands; after they evade 17,000 American troops sent after them, they are eventually captured or killed.
1884	Establishment of reservation for the Northern Cheyennes in Montana.
1887	U.S. Congress passes the General Allotment Act that divides Indian reservations into separate parcels (allotments) for each family; Southern Cheyenne reservation is allotted in 1892; Northern Cheyenne reservation is allotted in 1926.
1934	U.S. Congress passes the Indian Reorganization Act that gives funds for Indian reservations to buy back land that had been lost to outsiders; IRA also sets up tribal councils that have limited powers of self-government.
1947	U.S. Congress passes the Indian Claims Act that enables tribes to sue the federal government for land illegally lost or for land that had been sold at illegally low prices.
1961	Court of Indian Claims awards Southern and Northern Cheyennes $23 million in payment for land sold to the U.S. government in 1865 at prices well below the fair market value of the time.
1960s	Discovery of deposits of 5 billion tons of coal on the Northern Cheyenne reservation in Montana.

GLOSSARY

Algonquian. A language family that includes the Cheyenne language.

band. A grouping of people who form a stable community.

Council of Forty-Four. The governing body of peace chiefs of the Cheyennes. The Council has forty-four members, headed by a respected leader called the Sweet Medicine Chief.

culture. The way of life followed by a group of people, including their work, family structure, social rules, political system, and religious beliefs.

General Allotment Act. A law passed by Congress in 1887 that divided Native American reservations into separate parcels (allotments) of 160 acres for each family.

Indian Claims Act. A law passed by Congress in 1947 that enabled Native American reservations to sue the government for lands that had been illegally taken from them or for additional payment for lands that had been sold for illegally low prices.

Indian Reorganization Act. A law passed by Congress in 1934 that gave funds to Native American reservations to buy back land they had lost in previous years. The act also enabled reservations to set up tribal councils elected by residents.

pemmican. A preserved food made from dried buffalo meat mixed with dried berries.

reservation. An area of land owned by a group of Native American people.

Sacred Medicine Arrow Renewal. A four-day ritual held each summer to renew the Sacred Medicine Arrows and all of the Cheyenne Nation.

tanning. A process of softening animal hides (buffalo, deer, elk) so that they can be made into clothing, bedding, housing, and containers.

tepee. The house structure of the Cheyennes. Tepees are cone-shaped dwellings made from buffalo hides fastened to poles set in the ground in a circle and tapered at the top.

treaty. A legal agreement signed between two nations.

Tribal Council. The legal body of government on a reservation.

BIBLIOGRAPHY

*for children

Grinnell, George. *The Cheyenne Indians: Their History and Ways of Life.* 2 volumes. New York: Cooper Square Publishers, 1962.

Hoebel, E.A. *The Cheyennes: Indians of the Plains.* New York: Holt, Rinehart, & Winston, 1960.

*Hoig, Stan. *The Cheyenne.* New York: Chelsea House Publishers, 1989.

*———. *People of the Sacred Arrow.* New York: Dutton Children's Books, 1992.

Jablow, Joseph. *The Cheyenne in Plains Indian Trade Relations 1795–1840.* Seattle: University of Washington Press, American Ethnological Society Monograph #19, 1950.

Lowie, Robert. *Indians of the Plains.* Garden City, NY: Natural History Press, 1960.

*Meyers, Arthur. *The Cheyenne.* New York: Franklin Watts, 1992.

Stands-in-Timber, John, and Margot Liberty. *Cheyenne Memories.* New Haven: Yale University Press, 1967.

INDEX

Page numbers in *italics* refer to illustrations.